12.95
6/87

DATE D

What happens when you

HURT YOURSELF?

WHAT HAPPENS WHEN. . .?

What Happens When You Breathe?
What Happens When You Catch a Cold?
What Happens When You Eat?
What Happens When You Grow?
What Happens When You Hurt Yourself?
What Happens When You Listen?
What Happens When You Look?
What Happens When You Run?
What Happens When You Sleep?
What Happens When You Talk?
What Happens When You Think?
What Happens When You Touch and Feel?

Library of Congress Cataloging-in-Publication Data

Richardson, Joy.
  What happens when you hurt yourself?
  (What happens when — ?)
  Bibliography: p.
  Includes index.
  Summary: Describes what happens when the body sustains an injury
and how it heals itself.
  1. Wounds and Injuries — Juvenile literature. [1. Wounds and
injuries] I. Maclean, Colin, 1930-   ill.   II. Maclean, Moira, ill.
III. Title.   IV. Series: Richardson, Joy. What happens when — ?
  RD93.R53   1986   617'.1   86-3678
  ISBN 1-55532-132-1
  ISBN 1-55532-107-0 (lib. bdg.)

This North American edition first published in 1986 by
Gareth Stevens, Inc.
7221 West Green Tree Road   Milwaukee, Wisconsin 53223, USA

U.S. edition, this format, copyright © 1986
Supplementary text copyright © 1986 by Gareth Stevens, Inc.
Illustration copyright © 1983 by Colin and Moira Maclean

First published in the United Kingdom by Hamish Hamilton Children's
Books with an original text copyright by Joy Richardson.

Typeset by Ries Graphics, ltd.
Series editor: MaryLee Knowlton
Cover design: Gary Moseley
Additional illustration/design: Laurie Shock

What happens when you

HURT YOURSELF?

Joy Richardson

pictures by
Colin and Moira Maclean

introduction by
Gail Zander, Ph.D.

Gareth Stevens Publishing
Milwaukee

. . .a note to parents and teachers

Curiosity about the body begins shortly after birth when babies explore with their mouths. Gradually children add to their knowledge through sight, sound, and touch. They ask questions. However, as they grow, confusion or shyness may keep them from asking questions, and they may acquire little knowledge about what lies beneath their skin. More than that, they may develop bad feelings about themselves based on ignorance or misinformation.

The *What Happens When . . . ?* series helps children learn about themselves in a way that promotes healthy attitudes about their bodies and how they work. They learn that their bodies are systems of parts that work together to help them grow, stay well, and function. Each book in the series explains and illustrates how one of the systems works.

With the understanding of how their bodies work, children learn the importance of good health habits. They learn to respect the wonders of the body. With knowledge and acceptance of their bodies' parts, locations, and functions, they can develop a healthy sense of self.

This attractive series of books is an invaluable source of information for children who want to learn clear, correct, and interesting facts about how their bodies work.

GAIL ZANDER, Ph.D.
CHILD PSYCHOLOGIST
MILWAUKEE PUBLIC SCHOOLS

Oooh! Ouch!
If you cut your finger
or scrape your knee,
it hurts!

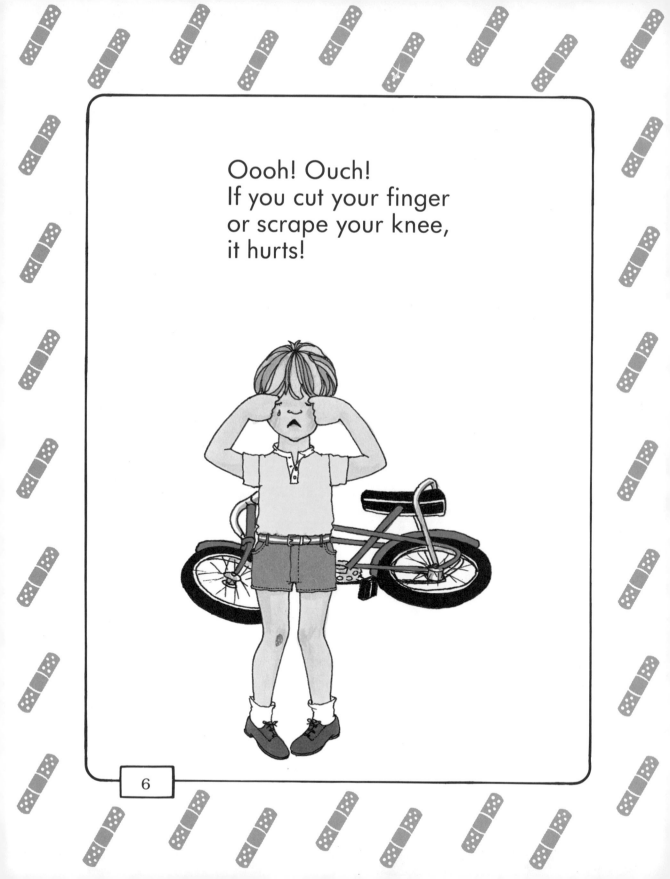

Under your skin
there are little threads
called nerves.
They tell you about
the things you touch.
This helps to stop you from
hurting yourself.

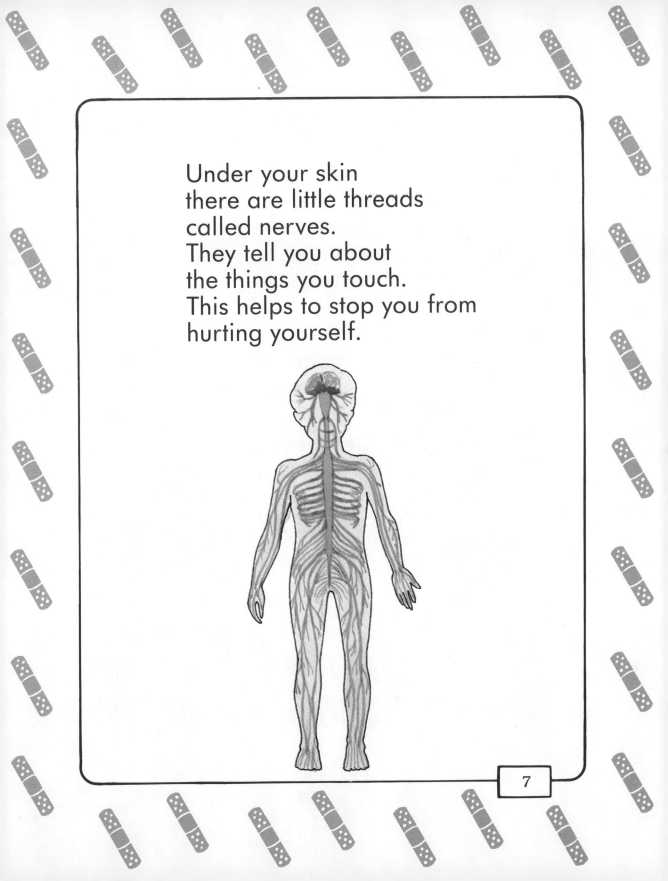

Choose six things
made of different materials
(like wood, paper, cardboard,
metal, plastic, and cloth).
Blindfold a friend and let her
feel the six things.
Can she tell what they are
and what they are made of?

Your nerves send messages to your brain
about all the things you touch.

If you touch something
sharp or hot, messages run
along the nerves to your brain
and your muscles.
You pull your hand away quickly.

Thin tubes called blood vessels
carry blood around your body.
If you cut yourself,
blood vessels in your skin
are cut open.
You bleed.

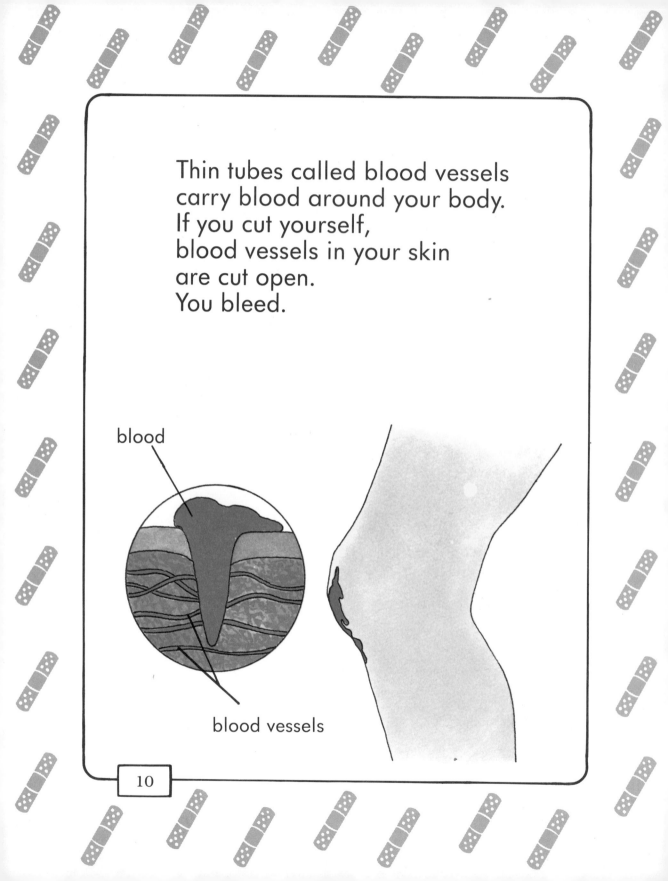

blood

blood vessels

Press hard on the back of your hand
with one finger.
Let go.
What do you notice?

Your skin gets lighter because
the blood cannot get through.
If you press on a cut,
the blood vessels are squashed.
The bleeding stops.

The cut slowly heals itself.
Drops of blood stick together.
They make a clot like glue
over the cut.
The clot hardens
and makes a scab.

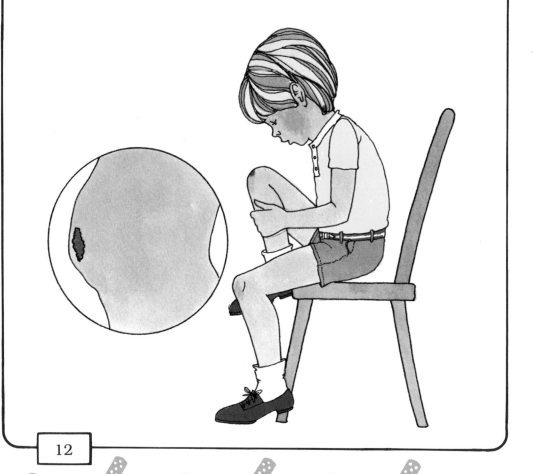

New skin grows under the scab.
When the cut is filled in,
the scab falls off.
It leaves a scar.
The new skin grows thicker.
Slowly the scar fades.
Serious cuts may leave
permanent scars.

If the cut is very bad,
the doctor may put stitches in it.
The stitches hold the sides together
while the cut heals.
The doctor uses a special needle
and thread to make the stitches.

Sometimes, instead of stitches the
doctor may use a special kind of
staples or bandage to hold the cut
together.

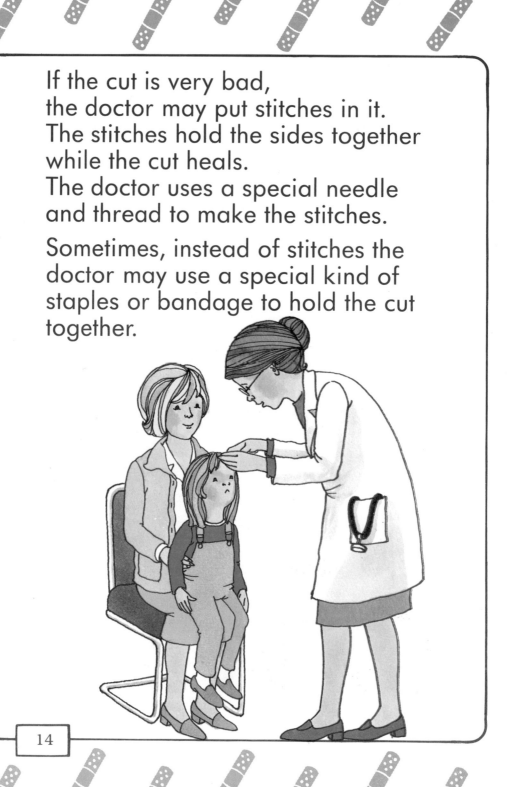

Make a cut
in a piece of thick cloth.
Can you stitch the sides together
with doctor's stitches?
They look like this.

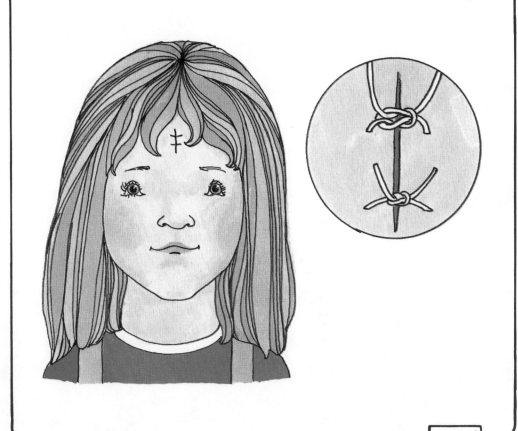

Cuts and scrapes
can let germs in.

Your blood looks red,
but it is made of
red cells and white cells
and watery liquid.
The white cells fight germs
and gobble them up.

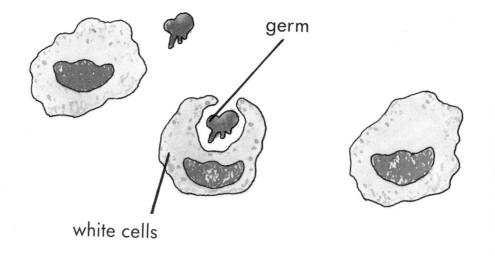

germ

white cells

Sometimes yellowy stuff called pus
oozes out of a cut.
It is made of dead white cells
and germs.
It shows there has been a fight
between them.

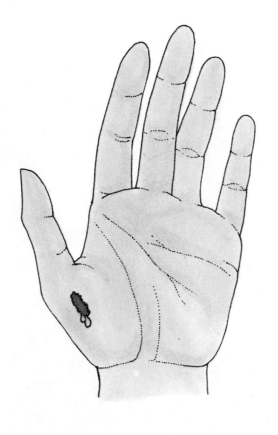

If you put a bandage
over a cut,
it keeps the cut clean and
helps to stop the bleeding.
Antiseptic can help to kill the germs.
Your body does the rest.

Can you find a place
where you have had a
cut or scrape?
Look at it closely
with a magnifying glass.

Can you see a scab or a scar,
or is it all healed?

19

If you fall,
you may bruise yourself.
Your skin does not break,
but the blood vessels
under the skin are hurt.

Blood leaks out
under your skin.
It makes a dark-colored bruise.

If the bruise is around your eye,
it is called a black eye.

Slowly the blood soaks back
into the blood vessels.

The bruise changes color.
It turns grey. Then it turns yellow.
Then it disappears.

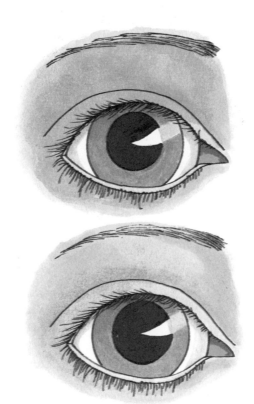

Drop an apple onto a hard floor.
Can you see the bruise?
Leave it for a few hours,
and then cut it open.
What has happened?

The hard bump damaged the flesh
and made a bruise.
A bruised apple cannot get
better again, the way you can.

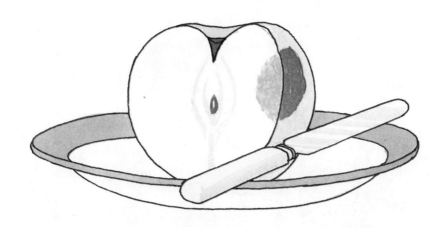

If your shoes rub your feet,
you may get a blister.
The blood vessels let out
some clear, watery liquid.
It makes a bulge
under your skin.

If the blister pops,
the watery liquid comes out.
The old skin dries up
and peels off.
New skin grows underneath.

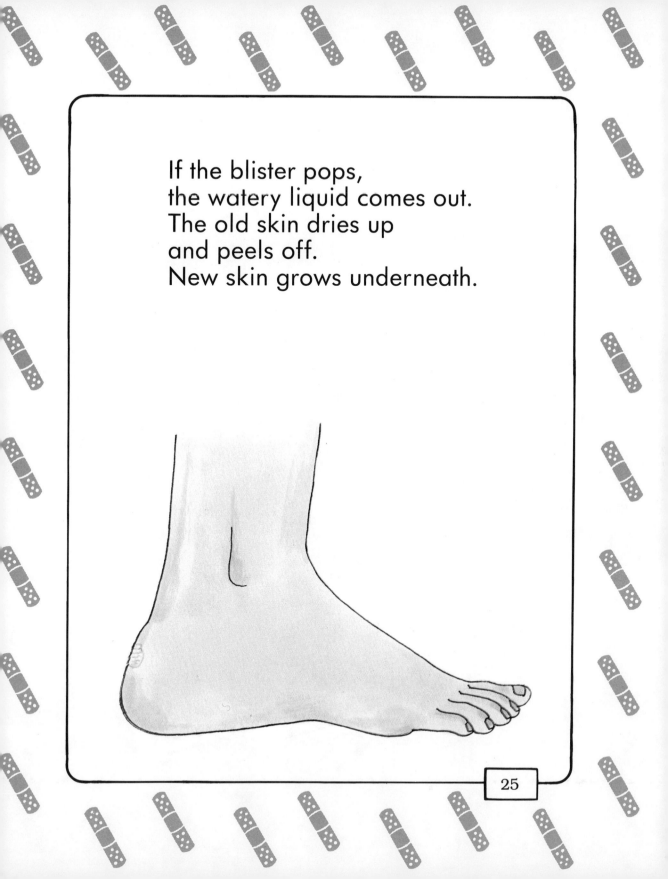

If you have a very bad fall,
you may break a bone.

The doctor takes
a special kind of photograph
called an X-ray
to see what has happened.

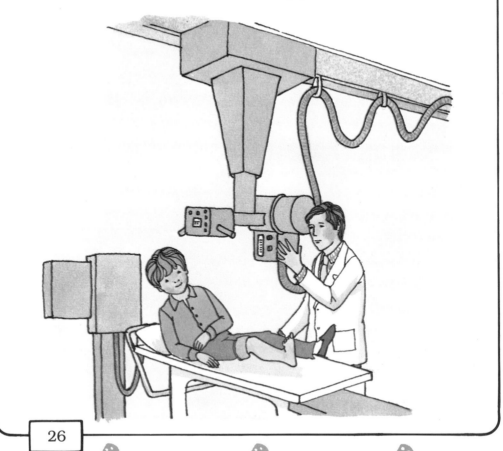

The doctor puts a cast
around the broken bone.
It keeps the bone straight
while it is healing.

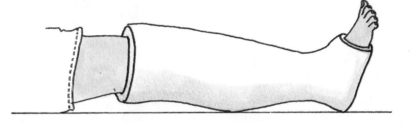

If your collarbone is broken,
a sling will help to keep it still.
(Your collarbone runs between
your neck and your shoulder.)
Can you make a sling like this
from a large square of cloth?

Soft, new bone grows in the gap
between the broken ends
and joins them up again.
The new bone gets harder until
the bone is as strong as it was before.

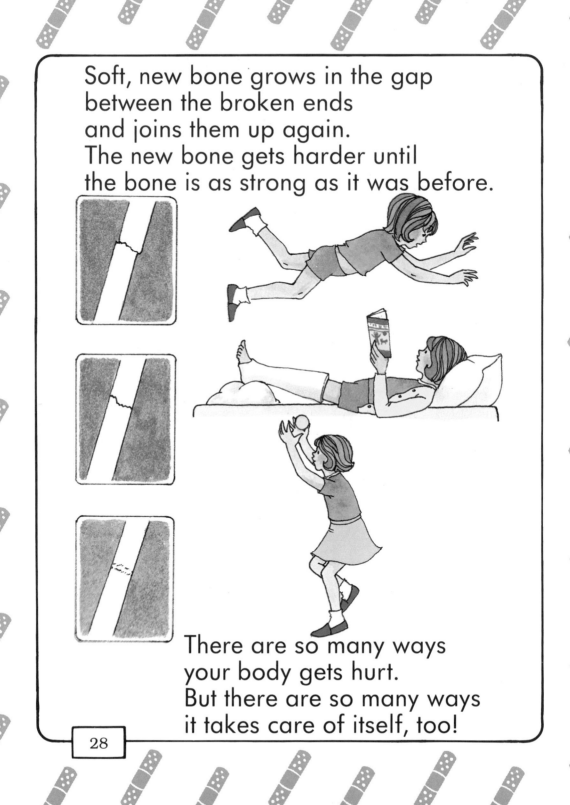

There are so many ways
your body gets hurt.
But there are so many ways
it takes care of itself, too!

How Does That Happen?

Did you find all these things to do in *What Happens When You HURT YOURSELF?* If not, turn back to the pages listed here and have some fun seeing how your body works.

1. See how your nerves send messages. (page 8)
2. Block off your blood vessels. (page 11)
3. Make doctor's stitches. (page 15)
4. Check out an old cut or scrape. (page 19)
5. See how an apple bruises. (page 23)
6. Make a sling. (page 27)

More Books About Getting Hurt

Listed below are more books about what happens when you hurt yourself. If you are interested in them, check your library or bookstore.

The Emergency Room. Rockwell (Macmillan)
From Head to Toes: How Your Body Works. Packard (Simon & Schuster)
The Hospital Book. Howe (Knopf)
A Hospital Story. Stein (Walker)
Matches, Lighters, and Firecrackers Are Not Toys. Chlad (Childrens Press)
Stay Safe, Play Safe: A Book About Safety Rules. Seuling (Western)
Things to Know Before You Go to the Doctor. Marsoli (Silver Burdett)
Things to Know Before You Go to the Hospital. Marsoli (Silver Burdett)
Thingumajig Book of Health and Safety. Keller (Childrens Press)
A Visit to the Sesame Street Hospital. Hautzig (Random House/Children's Television Workshop)
What to Do When Your Mom or Dad Says, "Be Careful!" Berry (Living Skills)
When I Cross the Street. Chlad (Childrens Press)
Will You Cross Me? Kaye (Harper & Row)

Where to Find More About Getting Hurt

Here are some people you can write away to for more information about what happens when you hurt yourself. Be sure to tell them exactly what you want to know about. Include your full name and address so they can write back to you.

Gerber Products Company
Fremont, Michigan 49412

Johnson and Johnson Products, Inc.
501 George Street
New Brunswick, New Jersey 08903

National Safety Council
425 North Michigan Avenue
Chicago, Illinois 60611

Index